Six Lines from Prison

Letters
of Nooshabeh Amiri
and Houshang Asadi

Dracopis Press

www.dracopis.com
beard@dracopis.com

DRACOPIS
dp
PRESS

Dracopis_004
Nooshabeh Amiri and Houshang Asadi: Six Lines from Prison

ISBN 978-91-87341-06-9
© 2013 Dracopis Press
The book is translated from Farsi
First edition. All rights reserved
Published by Dracopis Press, Sweden, 2013
EUROPE: Printed by Lightning Source, UK, 2013
USA: Printed by Lightning Source, USA, 2013

The prison correspondences of Nooshabeh Amiri and Houshang Asadi
were first published in Persian in 2003 by Éditions Kharavan in France,
under the title *Az Eshq va az Omid: Namehha-ye Zendan* (1361-1367)
[On Love and Hope: Prison Correspondences (1982-1988)].
A second edition in Persian, with a foreword and footnote commentary
by Ms. Amiri, was published in 2011 by Mardomak Publishing in the UK,
under the title *Shesh Khat az Zendan* [Six lines from Prison].
The Dracopis Press edition of *Six Lines from Prison* is the first English
translation of the letters, along with additional footnotes, a revised
foreword and a new afterword by Nooshabeh Amiri.

This publication was made possible through
the support of the Swedish Academy.

SIX LINES FROM PRISON

Foreword

Nooshabeh Amiri

It was February 6, 1983, and still two days left to the anniversary of our marriage. We had planned to go shopping the next day. We had tidied up our house and listed the things that we needed: several plates, some spoons, and glasses. We could get some of these from our friends. We didn't need any chairs as most of our guests didn't mind sitting on the floor. Parvaneh would sing and we hummed with her: "Winter comes to an end / Spring will bloom and ascend." With each refrain spring came closer. We had sung this particular song so many times that we started to believe in its message.

Early in the morning someone rang the bell. Houshang jump-started. The heavy thud of footsteps could be heard. Half awake, I heard the door of the apartment open. The sound of whispers was followed by a silence that spread like venom through my body. When Houshang returned to the room, his shoulders were drooping. His nostrils flared when he attempted to give me an explanation. This was an indication that he was hiding something from me: "Oh! Nothing, really." And upon my insistence: "They've been arrested."

We had feared our arrest for some time. Only a few nights before I had dreamt that Houshang had been arrested. Much like Samantha in the TV-series *Bewitched*, with a twitch of my nose, I tried to release him from the claws of his captors; I *was* able to get him off the hook but I had been so frightened that I couldn't escort him to a safe place. He fell into the fountain in the middle of Ferdowsi Square in central Tehran. This is when I woke up, still twitching my nose to fish him out of the fountain. In reality, this was taking place and I wasn't Samantha. "What should we do," I asked Houshang. "We'll leave town," he replied immediately. He said it in a way that worried me. I knew that in times of crises he had no control over himself. He would panic. He would come to his senses soon but at first he invariably had a knee-jerk reaction.

I suddenly remembered that I was supposed to pick up Manuchehr. He was one of the leaders of the Tudeh Party.[1] He had lived in Eastern Europe for many years before coming back to Iran with his German wife and two daughters, following the 1979 Revolution. It had been several months since his wife and daughters had returned to Germany. Everyone could smell danger in the air. Several days a week I would drive him from his house to his office. Suddenly fearing that they might also have arrested him, I rushed to pick him up at his house. I told Houshang that I would return once I had given Manuchehr a ride, to decide on what to do next.

---

1 Tudeh Party was one the most influential communist organizations in Iran. Formed in 1941 with pro-Soviet sympathies after the Allied occupation of Iran, it played an important role at major junctures in Iranian political history, including during the premiership of Mohammad Mossadeq (1951-1953). After the coup (1953) that toppled the administration of Mossadeq, Tudeh Party cadre and sympathizers were put behind bars. Some high-ranking members left the country to form an entity of resistance abroad. With the 1979 Revolution, these members could return to give renewed vigor to the Party, only to be persecuted, prosecuted, and at times executed in the years to come.

I dressed quickly and jumped behind the wheels of my white Toyota. "We don't have a minute to lose," I told my faithful wheels. We have to be on time for our rendezvous. I saw Manuchehr from a distance, his head hanging heavy on his shoulders, low in spirits and sad, looking into the distance. Not quite settled in the car, I told him the news of the arrest. I saw death cast a shadow over his eyes, as if the world was about to implode. There was a silence and then he said: "Let's go."

He didn't say a word along the way. "Please be careful," he turned around to tell me as he was getting out of the car. He grabbed my hand for a second and then let it go in a gesture of farewell. I realized, looking at the way he walked away, that he was sure he would never again see the light of day. My heart sank. I closed my eyes and led a finger under my eye to dab the tear that moistened my eyelashes. I allowed my head to sink into the headrest.

I heard knocks on the window. "Are you waiting for someone, Sister?" a voice asked. The "Sister" designation, used by religious revolutionary ideologists, sent shudders down my spine. "No! No!" I quickly pulled myself together and started the car. When I reached home, they had arrested Houshang. My mother was crying. "May Allah not forgive you if you harm this boy," she had told those who had come to take him away. "Don't worry, Mother," they had answered her, "it will only be for a couple of hours."

I tried to console my mother (whom Houshang and I called Mamani). Then I left the house to pay a visit to Rahman, who was once our editor at *Keyhan*. The famous "THE SHAH LEFT" and "THE IMAM ARRIVED" headlines were his handiwork.[2] Mass arrests had terrorized activists and the stench of it had also permeated his house. "They came for Rahman early in the morning," his wife said, "but released him later." She continued: "He called me but I don't know where he is now. He may not come back home." I collapsed on the couch crying. Rahman was a role model for me and I felt lost without him. I had to get out even though I didn't know where I was going. I made several calls from the public phone. Many of those calls were not picked up. Some would say, for example, "Behruz has gone to the hospital" or "Fati had food poisoning and is now in the emergency ward." These were codes that they had been arrested as well. Now I was even scared to drive within the city. Behind every street light I feared being boarded and arrested. It was not uncommon that relatives of political prisoners where arrested. I tried not to look people in the eyes. I returned home in the evening, climbed the stairs two at a time to reach our apartment. Mamani was sitting anxiously, waiting for the door to open. And there is nothing worse than seeing a helpless mother waiting for some news about her daughter, not knowing whether or not she had been arrested.

Hours were passing without any news from Houshang. Confused and disoriented I fell to my bed. The blow was

---

2 *Keyhan* and *Etela'at* are two wide-circulation newspapers whose managing editors after the Revolution have been assigned by the Supreme Leader of Iran. *Keyhan* was and remains the bastion of hard-knuckle politics. The chief editor of *Keyhan* is a much feared figure whose incendiary editorials are seen as policy-setters and a sign of things to come. *Etela'at*, on the other hand, is run by a more moderate editor.

incomprehensible. I knew my hopes. I was still in love with spring. I had yet to be taught hatred. It was time to get out, to hit the streets. I went home to Rahman's mother. Her house used to be a hangout. She was such a kind soul. During the 1979 Revolution, we would go to her after street demonstrations, to be served cutlets and fresh bread. She later succumbed to Alzheimer's. One day, without anyone knowing how, she went to her old neighborhood and sat outside her childhood home. May she rest in peace.

Rahman's wife was there, along with her mother, Azizjaan. Unsuspecting, Rahman's little daughter was in her own world. I was now officially a prisoner's wife and Rahman's wife was waiting to become one. She had been expecting this title for years—much prior to the Revolution of 1979. There was no news of Rahman.

I left the house and drove without knowing where to go. It was late. "It will only be for a couple of hours," they had said, "to answer a few short questions." I was still in a daze but I knew that "a couple of hours" was a joke. "A few questions" was a lie. From this moment on I started a harrowing struggle to keep hope alive. This struggle continued for six years and two weeks. Hardly a couple of hours.

I no longer had dreams. I just went from one civil servant to another. Blisters covered my feet. I had written to all the people that might have connections. I made an appointment with the Head of the Parliament. He listened in silence as I kept explaining. At last he said: "This is a situation that we simply cannot get involved in." I told him he better help us now or soon it'll be their turn to face the music. He knew this, but didn't care to get into the fray.[3]

I made an appointment with a Member of the Parliament. He was a young man who also wrote for the newspaper *Etela'at*, where I had come across a paragraph in which he proclaimed: "Through kindness thorns turn into flowers." My reply to him was: "Does writing turn anything into anything?" He also listened to what I had to say and sympathized, but was incapable of doing anything. No one did anything.

A year and two months elapsed in relative darkness. There were the rare telephone calls. I began dreaming again, well, more like nightmares. Prisoners were lined up against a blue backdrop—suspended for the televised confessions—to defame themselves on camera: "I am anti-revolutionary, a spy... A spy for the CIA, a spy for Mossad..." Everything appeared as it would on a TV-screen—every now and then, the state-run television turned the screen into a confessional, and showcased a number of people belonging to various political groups; lined up against a blue backdrop they admitted to having been duped, describing how they had slipped and sold their souls to the Devil. The stories of their digression were exact duplicates of each other.

There was no phone in the house. Every time I heard

---

3 The post-revolutionary order suppressed activities of political parties in a manner that clearly forebode a grim future for all kinds of political activity. The purges started with Marxists, liberals, and leftists, and slowly extended to include more progressive organizations within the ruling power. The presidential election of 2009 was the ultimate showdown between fundamentalist and reformist elements within the Islamic Republic of Iran—which led to the house arrest of reformist candidates Mir Hossein Moussavi (former post-revolutionary prime minister, 1981-1989) and Mehdi Karoubi (former parliamentary chairman, 2000-2004) following a much contested vote count that reinstated the incumbent Mahmoud Ahmadinejad as president.

the buzzer, shivers ran down my back. Many were now wallowing in fresh blood, and each one after sitting in front of that blue backdrop. When would that backdrop shroud my beloved? How would our days continue away from each other? What did these people intend to do to the blue sky?

I took refuge in the poetry of Hafez and Rumi. I had read the letters of Imam Ali to his governor Malik al-Ashtar so often that I knew them by heart.[4] This I thought was necessary, because in official communications quoting from these letters could prove pivotal when attempting to gain ground with pious officials. But still no one was willing to do anything. Our little house was quiet. Lifeless.

The evening before Nowruz—the Iranian New Year—in 1984 the door bell rang. I jump-started. A friend came in with a piece of good news: "They called our house and said that at 3 pm tomorrow we should show up at Felestin Street, where the old Swiss School was, for a visit... a VISIT... a VISIT! They said that we could only take a box of pastries with us... pastries... PASTRIES... PASTRIES!" I heard words in waves and echoes. After a year and two months, I was to see my husband, the one who had been taken away for a simple Q&A, and who was supposed to come back in no time at all.

I was driving my steadfast Toyota, and my mother, who had not left my side, was sitting next to me. Traffic was dense. It was five minutes to 3 pm. I looked around the street. It would be impossible to make it in this

---

4 These letters are instructions on governance by the 4th Caliph after the advent of Islam, and are collected in the book *Nahj ul-Balagha*.

traffic. I had to walk the rest of the way. I turned the engine off. "I am leaving," I said to no one in particular, "tell the driver behind us to come and move the car…" and then I ran.

The mandatory veil became entangled around my feet and ankles. The pastry box in my hands was a precious gift. They had said that we were allowed to bring no more than a kilogram. I had asked the pastry shop clerk to put a sample of everything in the box—almonds, peanuts, sugar candy, and pastries. In the past fourteen months, without my companion, all that I had eaten had tasted bitter like poison, wondering whether he was eating proper meals or not, with that delicate stomach of his, with his headaches. Whenever I enjoyed the brilliant sunshine, the freshness of a breeze, or the flow of water, I had wondered what my soul mate was going through. Had prison kept the sun from him? Could guards block the breeze from coming in? Had he forgotten the sound of a water stream?

I entered the former school yard with several other families. Our husbands, our fathers, our sons were all in blue uniforms, lined up against the wall. There was a moment of silence. And then arrested emotions erupted in tears. They took our ID's and then called us in by turns. At the far end of the yard there were a few rooms with classroom desks. At those desks, on that day, the prisoners sat with their families.

My turn came. They called me in. My heart was about to come undone. When I walked to the visiting rooms I passed a veranda where an older man in prison garb said hello. I didn't recognize him at first, but then, his kind eyes reminded me how tense I was. I hesitated.

Was I to return his greeting? Or should I be more cautious? It could have brought unwanted consequences for him. Maybe it wouldn't be good for me either. Fear can simply permeate our every thought. I greeted him with my eyes.

A guard summoned me to another part of the room. In fact, he pushed me. "Move," he ordered. I did, in silence, unquestioningly. I saw a walking "sack" wrapped in rags, with a long beard and yellow skin. I reckoned it was just another prisoner, but he came my way with open arms. I couldn't believe it. He was my 34-year old husband. I flew to his arms. "Wait!" someone ordered and then whispered a few commands to another guard. One of the guards came and stood next to me. Another one next to my husband. And we laid our heads on each others' shoulders under a pair of watchful eyes, to shed tears.

They sat us on either side of the classroom desk. A "Brother" sat between my husband and I, possibly to listen in, not knowing that at times of desolation and calamity nothing worth any ear will pass the mouths.

Fifteen minutes later we were told that the meeting had come to an end. And everyone heeded the commandment like robots. We left and our loved ones stayed.

I carried my fears, hatred and devastation outside the school, to the streets, and then the car. I couldn't believe what had befallen us in the very era of the Revolution. Who can claim, I reflected, that cars are less sensitive than so-called "Brothers", as my husband's captors were fond of calling each other—? My car even knows that it is not supposed to break down or play games. It is true that my car has been around, but it knows that I am devastated and sad. It always goes the distance with little left in the fuel tank. It's only when I take it to the repair shop that I realize my car is on the last drop of oil too.

* * *

Not even that kind of visit was repeated. Our only connection was over the phone, once every month. I went to a friend's house early in the morning and waited for his call. I showed up six in the morning and sat next to the phone, deeply embarrassed and apologetic for disturbing the peace of my friend's family. My host, of course, was extremely kind, but for how long could I rely on their hospitality? Every time the phone rang, I jumped. I didn't even know when exactly he would be allowed to call me, as only the days were known but no hour was set.

— Hi.

— Hi.

— How are you?

— Doing well.

And then it was over. I didn't share a single one of the thoughts I had prepared in my head. I couldn't. I was so overwhelmed by the deep sorrow I sensed in Houshang's voice and became tongue-tied. This continued for another year, almost in the same way, although I was not the same inculpable person. I no longer cried. I had become tougher by the day. I didn't even recognize myself any longer. The delicate glass surface of humanity was scratched.

I had returned to dubbing. I lip-synced for roaches and mice in—mostly—Japanese cartoons. I no longer enjoyed the job. I didn't care what viewers thought of my voice. I spoke with my husband through mice and roaches. I was also a prisoner—in the large jail on this end of the phone line.

It took from February 6, 1983 to April 1985—no less than two years and a few months—to be given permission to correspond once a month and have visits every other week. They had transferred my husband to Evin Prison. A month later the first letter arrived, dated 1985. It was an A4-sized sheet with neat lines dividing it into two sections. The upper section was where my husband could write—six lines only. The lower section was mine. This six-line affair continued for almost four years. Prison names changed—Qezel-Hesar, Gohar-Dasht, and Evin again—but the letter format was the same.[5]

---

5 Evin Prison in Northern Tehran is flanked by the towering Alborz Mountain Range. The construction began in 1961 and took ten years to complete—the prison extends over an area of 43 hectares. In Iran's political encyclopedia "Evin" is synonymous with torture and depredation, and it is where the mass executions of 1988 took place. Various entities of the security and intelligence apparatus of the Islamic Republic (the Revolutionary Guard or IRCG, the Revolutionary Prosecutor's Office, the Judiciary) had their own sections in the prison, each with its own protocols.

Qezel-Hesar is the largest and oldest prison, located in the Qezel-Hesar district of the city of Karaj, near Tehran. It was built prior to the 1979 Revolution, modeled after U.S. prisons for non-political prisoners. Under the Islamic Republic, Qezel-Hesar set aside three of its main wards for political prisoners. Political prisoners, however, changed the interior design of the cells. They planted flowers in the yard and convinced the ferocious prison chief, Hajj Davud, to allow them to use the agricultural plot of land behind the cells, which he did under the pretext of rehabilitating the prisoners.

Gohar-Dasht was among the prisons that where built in the 1970's. It is one of only two Iranian prisons modeled after Israeli prisons; the second being

I made a copy of most of the letters before sending them off. I don't know why. Perhaps because I always feared that I may not see Houshang again, and thus wanted to have a part of him for safekeeping. Making the copies was not to be carried out without misgivings. Fear was everywhere. Copying a letter with a prison letterhead could potentially bring about ominous consequences. I was haunted by all kinds of paranoia. Every time I went to the copy shop, I would put the letter between two ordinary documents, careful that the owner wouldn't notice the letterhead. Perhaps because of this awkward behavior, the shop owner would always come and offer to help me. On a couple of occasions, I darted out when he asked if I needed any assistance, leaving him in utter consternation.

The letters accumulated in my closet. Sometimes I would pull out a few and read them through, but the thought of publishing them never entered my mind. They were more like painful memories that had to be kept in the dark recesses of the house. It was when Seyyed Mohammad Khatami became president[6] I first thought of publishing them. I spoke to a publisher and she even offered a progressive way of distributing the book—directly to bookstores, without any of the ordinary wholesalers. The letters were retyped, the book

---

Adel-Abad in the city of Shiraz. Most of the prisoners' quarters in this system are small solitary cells with completely white walls, always with fluorescent light, and toilets inside the cells. Food is pushed through small openings at the bottom of the main door.

6 In a landslide victory August 2, 1997, Mohammad Khatami became the fifth president of the Islamic Republic of Iran. "The second of Khordad"—the date of his election according to the Persian calendar—became a milestone in Iran's political history and marked the formation of the reform movement.

got outlined, and the cover was designed at the offices of the magazine *Gozaresh Film* ("Film Report"). I was filled with emotions each time I read over the letters. The colleague who retyped the letters did her job quietly. She was pious and each day performed her prayers on the premises. Sometimes I would see her cry in silence. One day, I saw tears roll down the cheeks of the cover designer. Both of them were young and had not witnessed any events of the early Revolutionary era, but tried to comprehend it all through the turbulence of the Reform era after Khatami had taken office. Another day, one of the two advised me in whispers, "I wish you will be more careful now," realizing the sufferings that Houshang and I had endured.

Even before its publication, the book whipped up great interest. The publisher had placed an ad in a book review magazine. Based on advance orders she had concluded that it would sell several thousand copies. We were happy to have been able to publish our writings about the flames of love surviving the time of cholera.

But then there came a phone call from the Ministry of Culture and Islamic Guidance (in short called Ershad ["Guidance"] among Iranians). And the publisher explained to us that the censors now had objected to parts of the book. I was shocked. They were revoking the permission that they earlier had granted us.

Finally one day, the publisher and I went to the Ershad offices. The head of the pertinent bureau was a professed reformist but, as it turned out, far from reform-minded: "Get rid of all the commentary and you can get a printing permission." I was beside myself: "Sir, just today the letter of Emadeddin Baqi's 13-year old daughter was published, and she had a lot more pointed content than there is in my annotations for this book. Why should I get rid of simple explanations?" Without batting an eyelash he said: "Because Emadeddin Baqi is one of *us*."[7]

By the time we got out of the Ershad building I ran a fever. The pain of this rejection was unbearable. The book was not to come out. The following years a storm hit the world of Iranian letters.

In 2001 the editorial office of *Gozaresh Film* was shut down. Houshang and I went to France for a couple of months to let things settle. It was in this period we became acquainted with the director of a publishing house. We had lunch together and made arrangements for the book to come out in Persian in Paris. We then returned to Iran.

For the book we wrote an introduction on behalf of the publisher, to avoid any kind of unwanted consequences. And in 2003 the letters were finally published. By then we were living in France permanently. A new Persian edition came out in the UK in 2011. The original explanatory notes (from the time we were trying to do the book with *Gozaresh Film*) could now be updated and elaborated for inclusion.

---

7 Emadeddin Baqi is a former IRGC member, who in the late 1990's joined the reformist ranks as an investigative journalist and later became a human rights and prisoner's rights advocate. He spent time in prison for his reports on the Chain Murder of Intellectuals. While in prison, reformist newspapers published letters that his daughter, Maryam, and his wife, Fatemeh Kamali, had written to him.

One Letter a Month
Letters of 1364
[May 1985-March 1986]

Nooshabeh Amiri & Houshang Asadi

Letter I

My very good wife, once a month we have the opportunity to write. You can write me back on this very paper and send it to the address below. I hope you are doing well. I won't say how much I miss our beautiful life. I am supposed to go to court any day now. You can be certain that these days will come to an end and I will return to the arms of my family and community. I count the seconds to see you and to receive your reply.

Hello my dear companion. Mamani and I are doing well. We are missing you and hoping for the day when you return home. I can only wish that in court, the person in charge will keep justice in mind when passing a sentence. I hope you regain your liberty very soon and come back to our little house. Let me assure you, just as I declared in my marriage vow, I shall be your partner forever. I shall love you, in good times and in bad, in sickness and in health.

Letter II

FROM PRISON
Grand lady of my love, I greet you. You are not just my love but my father, mother, sister, brother, friend, spouse… all of my existence. I have a place in my heart for you as large as all the expanses of the world extended in each direction. I count the seconds for that happy day when I return to our little house. Please give my warmest and most lavish kisses upon Mamani. I am ashamed of all the suffering that I have caused, but what can I do? Forgive me. Allah hasn't forgotten us, you said. I hope for the days of sadness to come to an end. With every breath I repeat, I LOVE YOU.

My Houshang, light of my abode, on this dark night the slightest suggestion of meeting you brings the light of day to my eyes. My dearest, without you my moments pass with difficulty, but they are also filled with the hope that the door of our house will one day open to receive you. My dear, Mamani and I are with you every second of the day and our minutes are spent hoping for your return. I am certain that Allah is watching our yearnings and that He will one day grant our wish to be together. Be hopeful and take care of yourself. Hoping for a day when all our sufferings will have come to an end. I love you very much.

Letter III

FROM PRISON

Hello my precious. My heart cries for you as much as all those sad autumn rains that you mentioned. I want to rest my head on your velvety shoulders and cry my heart out like all the wandering clouds in the grey autumnal sky. Without you I am a child lost in this big world. The sun is setting. Another day is added to our separation and we are a day closer to our reunion. I count the settings and risings of the sun and that which never sets in me is the radiating sun of your love. Sad but hopeful, I await a tomorrow when this sorrow will come to an end and your smile can bring springtime to our house. My darling, I wish I was there and had a share of all those pains that you carry on your delicate shoulders. I wish I could laugh, cry, and die with you. I wish I was never without you. I miss the song of your kindness in the small veranda of our house. Sad and hopeful, I don't doubt that these sufferings will come to an end. I love you as much as the extent of your kindness, and await the moment I can lay eyes on you.

FROM HOME

My breath, my husband, I miss you like all the autumns and springs that come and go. I miss being with you. You are the embodiment of love and joy, of humanity, and I love all these characteristics in you. My love, we have been introduced to suffering; no wonder we understand love and cherish it profoundly.[8] My shoulders may be delicate, but I want you to know that they get their strength from the power of our love. My eyes may be moist, but they are staring the suffering down. As long as there is hope, there is life, and when love is added to the mix, humans become stronger yet. Do not worry, these days shall soon come to an end. Our little house will again be filled with sparkle and light, and the sparrows perched on our poplar tree will one day sing: "This flame was kept alive." And this living flame is the flame of our beautiful life. I know our situation is difficult and morbid, but I also know that it will come to an end. It is for the sake of that future I have let this flame dance in the wind of today. I love you. Don't worry and take care of yourself.

---

8 It is not easy to elaborate feelings in a short letter. To overcome the space limitation, we had to appeal to shared memories and experiences. In this entry, I am referring to a poem by Rahman Hatefi, where he says: "We have been introduced to love / And understood suffering." It might be hard to fully grasp the strong sentiment that could rise in us by evoking the name of a writer friend like Rahman Hatefi.

Letter IV

FROM PRISON

Grand lady of my love, I kiss the vast forehead of your loving kindness. My darling, I wanted to write about the pungent taste of loneliness, of the bone-chilling cold of the fourth winter of our separation, of the dark days without you, when, behold, your letter arrived.[9] The hopeful melancholy of your words brought spring-time to my sky. Flowers started to bloom. Birds began to sing. Your teary eyes danced before mine. They wept and you laughed, just like the sun coming out while rain is falling. I grew from the rainbow of your smile and arced for the sky. I picked the stars of your tears and was filled with hope and music. My kind lady, I extend my hand now, braced by the warmth of your love, hoping for a bright future. Receive me, give me shelter, I am hopeful. The flower of joy will soon bloom in our house and I will breathe the air of that day with the thought of you in my mind. I sing the song of I LOVE YOU again and again. Kiss lovely Mamani all over her face. I kiss the motherly folds of her skin. I love you as much as love itself.

---

9 Houshang was arrested in winter time, and was set free six years later in another winter, so we were apart for seven winters.

My Houshang, companion of my moments, with the approach of the anniversary of your incarceration, I am enveloped in an even more profound sadness. I miss spending time with you. My eyes are fixed on the road and my heart beats for that moment when our door will open to frame you. As you can sense, I am sad but hopeful. This is a hope tall as the body of love, towering as all cypresses and poplars, strong as faith. Darling! We celebrated your birthday with and without you again. I repeated your name and wished you happy birthday, reminding myself time and again: "Never shall she die, the one whose heart is filled with love."[10] My husband, know that I share your joys and sorrows, in the gray sundown of your prison cell, lamenting the shadow of those distancing bars. I am always with you and gain strength from the strength and clarity of our love. My hands are in yours and yours are my support. We are invited to the banquet of tomorrow. It won't be too long before you arrive, and this hope is the padding of my life. It is as certain as the day that comes and the night that leaves. I love you my love, and loving is a powerful force. Mamani also loves you. Take care of yourself.

---

10 Proverbial stanza by 14th-century Persian mystic and poet Hafez.

Letter V

FROM PRISON

Grand lady of my love, with my autumnal heart I greet your vernal eyes. I clasp your hands from a distance and whisper the eternal hymn of I LOVE YOU. By the time you are reached by this letter, the eight anniversary of our marriage will have come to pass. On the day you wore that white dress our name was registered next to each other for ever amidst the teary eyes of Uncle Rahman, and three years have elapsed since our separation.[11] Before the day you came into my life for

---

11 Rahman Hatefi was our marriage witness. With those kind eyes, which always seemed to look into the distance, he had told us that life would be difficult, but he had also reminded us that human life was not simply an eating and sleeping machine. A year after the crackdown, Rahman was killed in prison. His wife came by on the day she had heard the news. A full account of this meeting will appear at another time, but the short of it is:

"A black dressed woman and a girl are standing in the middle of the street, looking at our house. What did I see? Shokuh, the Editor's wife. I flew down the stairs and reached the door. Shokuh was leaving. I cried: *It's me. I am here.* Shokuh turned around. She was broken. She staggered towards me like a robot. We were only a few meters apart when my heart sank: *Did they kill Houshang,* I thought to myself, and wondered if she was here to inform me of it. It didn't even occur to me that they may have arrested the editor as well. I was about to collapse on the ground when Shokuh grabbed my hand, and with a painful expression said: *They have killed Rahman.* We melted in each other's arms. We were crying and could hear the voice of 'Hajj Agha' from afar: *They must kill you all like dogs. Like a dog. A dog...* I don't know for how long we sat there and cried. Then, our tears suddenly went dry. The 13-year old daughter of Rahman had put her head in her mother's lap and gone to sleep. I managed to get some words out of the deep well of my throat. *When,* I asked, *and how.* Shokuh blurted out that they had just called earlier to say that he had committed suicide by chewing his veins. They had given her a reference number to present at the Behesht Zahra morgue. *I have come to ask you to go with me. I have no one left.* Each of her words—suicide, chewing veins, the morgue—sent electric shocks through my body. I cringed, trembled, and felt the pain reverberating through my body. I saw that I was

ever, I was a lost soul. Now, too, I am lost. I will be alone even if a thousand people surround me. My heart is missing a beat because my lady is not around. My autumnal heart is with me, rain or shine. But I am like a lost stranger in the fogged days of separation. A pair of teary eyes dance before my bedazzled gaze. Hands reach across from great distances to receive me. My whole existence rests on that moment when the wall of separation comes down. Beginning my journey towards 37, I know that I have only been happy for six years. Those are the years that I breathed with you. I salute that merry day. Celebrate our anniversary in the hope that we can do so together in the future. Kiss Mamani all over her face. I love you like love itself.

---

suspended in mid air, detached from everything."

My Houshang, man of my home, I honor your greetings and keep your love close to me, for no hearts can be as loving as ours. I repeat your love song with you and loudly recite the mating of our hearts. I want everyone to know that only lovers can suffer and remain in love—to suffer and love, to be separated and love more. My dear husband, on the anniversary of our marriage, I want you to know that I have marked the moments of being with you—even the past three years—as the most powerful moments of my existence. My life is grafted into your existence, to your name, to the human being that you are and I know. Yes, let me celebrate the anniversary of that day. Merrier still the day when the walls of separation come down and we can overcome suffering with the power of our love, and again let the song of life cascade like mountain springs. My darling, I beseech you: let hope warm your tender heart and push autumn gloom away. The essence of life is in the process of blooming. Autumns come and go, let's hold hand from distance and begin our flight across the land of hope. Our shield is our love and courage is our witness. I love you as much as there is vastness in hope.

Letter VI

Grand lady of my love, I greet you from my heart. By the time this letter will reach your hands, spring has come to the city. You know that no one can postpone the coming of spring. As such I once more, in this New Year when our separation gets renewed, greet the sun of your eyes.[12] I summon all the flowers of spring with your name. I sing your name with all the birds. Happy New Year to you! Happy springtime! I live with the hope of a spring spent with you. We can then celebrate, along with the trees of our little house, the blooming of flowers from the dark heart of the soil. From the bosom of your virtuous love our house will be filled with flowers. On the hour of the arrival of the New Year, I will salute you and the spring. I will arrange my *haftseen* in the wind.[13] You said my letters were sad. I declaim: "Every word in my letters emanates from an autumnal heart, in sadness as profound as your rainy eyes." It wouldn't have made sense otherwise. When you are not

---

12 Nowruz, the Iranian New Year, starts at the vernal equinox (end of March). In the Iranian plateaus this is marked by a total seasonal upheaval. In no less than a few days trees shoot off buds and grass grows green.

13 A tradition at Nowruz is to arrange a spread—either on a table or on the ground—with various items, seven of which start with the letter S in Persian: س. It is called "Haft-Seen" ([haft = seven] + [seen = the letter S]). Family members gather around haftseen at the hour of vernal equinox. The articles of haftseen can be chosen among these, each of which have their own symbolic meaning: *sīr* (garlic), *sīb* (apple), *sabzeh* (grass), *senjed* (oleaster), *serkeh* (vinegar), *samanu* (juice of germinating wheat or malt mixed with flour and brought to a consistency), *somaq* (sumac), *sonbol* (hyacinth), and/or *sekkeh* (a coin).

with me, when I can't hear your love song, when I can't smell the delicate scent of your kindness, when I close my eyes at night to a sight other than your visage, and open them without seeing your countenance, when the world and everything in it is uncanny, I must be mad not to feel sad. All the joy in this world is you. When you are not around, I can only wear a mask of happiness like a miserable clown. Oh! object of my devotion, this autumnal melancholy, this arid sadness, is not an indication of hopelessness. You are not with me, but I *am* you; hence, you *are*, in the way existence just is. You live in me though you are absent. As such, I am hopeful and warm in the heart. In the space between two visits, in this meandering icy patch of the road, I warm my heart with the warmth of your love, which penetrates windows and walls to touch me. I know that you will be standing tall at the end of these days, which will be the beginning of me—you will be standing. I call on you, my kind lady; give me your virtuous hand. I love you as much as all the blossoms of spring. Kiss Mamani all over her face.

FROM HOME

My Houshang, man of my home, I answer you from my heart. Yes, spring is breathing in the city, and with each inhalation and exhalation it sprinkles the scent of hope in our little house. I see you following the growth of lotuses in our garden and each morning I hear your voice announcing the blooming of yet another lotus.[14] And it is as such life can reveal its secrets—the lotus seed struggling with dark soil, and thus coming into flower. To me, you and our joint life is a manifestation of that flowering. Thereby I have been empowered to love. The love and the scents cannot be kept subdued. My love, I sense your sadness with all my heart. I share your every moment of sorrow, but I see spring knocking on your autumnal heart. My love, in the coming year, freedom will get closer. That way, every moment of this New Year becomes a celebration. The meanderings of

14 I have inherited the love of flowers from Mamani. To me a house is a home when there are flowers in it, those that I have planted myself and seen coming out of the ground. In the early days of the Revolution I wrote a story based on the blooming of a flower. Its unfinished petals had called for a meeting to vote for the "proper time" to greet the sun. Those were the days of youth, dream and idealism. I was inspired by watching the flowerbox on our balcony. Every spring, we would plant seeds of lotus and buttercup, and daily we would pay them a visit. Whenever we could spot a green sprout we would celebrate. In my new solitude I talked to the flowers and confided in them. I would take them, fresh or wilted, as signs of time. In this letter, I have written of such flowers. I never told Houshang that on the first year of his arrest, all the plants in our house died. The elm tree by our house suddenly transformed into a dead log. My heart died with them all. But it is also true that on the day Houshang was released, the cactus that I had planted brought forth a big, yellow flower, gazing at the dark days of the past; and also some zinnias could harangue their colorfulness, pride, and beauty.

this icy road will have an end, and a day will come when we are able to go over our memories. Today I proclaim, and will do so until the day you are no longer there and I am no longer here: I LOVE YOU. Mamani kisses you and has great hopes for you. Eventually we will get to our dreams. I know it.

Where Are Your Hands?
Letters of 1365
[April 1986-March 1987]

Nooshabeh Amiri & Houshang Asadi

Letter I

FROM PRISON

Lady, lady, my dear lady, once again my vernal heart greets your sunshine smile. I am not there with you when the flowers are blooming. What a shower of flora. All the nightingales are warbling. The bastards have come to celebrate your birthday with their chirps. And they sing with me, because our song is not in vain, because love is not in vain, because love is tomorrow, is eternity itself. I bring you all the love in this world, because everything seems small next to you. Your heart is tender, delicate and in love, like a butterfly. Your patience, your care, your faith are all exemplary. You wear the eastern sun on your sleeve. May the victory of love befit you! Where are your hands, my lady? Sing my song for I have a heavy heart among all these strangers. But I smile, because you come from the vernal sky and bring hope for a future where I may be with you, like this breeze that passes through my heart. Listen! Can you hear my heart calling for you? "Never shall he die / He whose heart beats with love."[15] When I write to you, I am just as sad and hopeful as all the sheets of paper in the world. But this is the last line for me in this sheet. I love you very much. I love you. Kiss my plump and kind Mamani.

---

15 Proverbial poem by Hafez.

My Houshang, my kind husband, I greet you. I greet you and your sufferings. I greet you and your hopes. I greet you as I greet the morrow. The flowers that I planted, my love, in our small flowerbox, on our small balcony, now have sprouted. This year, I have also planted a zinnia, which is a plant with only a few flowers. There is only a single flower at the top of each stem. It is somewhat like a narcissus, but comes in pink, purple, and red. Now, that's a sight to see! The flowers stand tall and have their eyes on the sun. In between them some lotuses have shot forth—turquoise, blue, and as pretty as love itself. Each morning I go to the lotuses and whisper to them—as if I was murmuring to you—before they fold their petals. Our flowers greet you as well, and they miss you in the house. But the sadness of your absence is also mixed with the hope of being with you. I speak to them and they to me. Our conversation always harks back to you. Darling, this year both doves and nightingales are keeping us company. We partake in our own ball—the flowers, nightingales and I—and you are the flame of our gathering. Also Mamani attends this festive gala, intoning the word "Houshang"—and she wishes you strength, happiness and health. Yes, as long as there is hope and love, our house will be bustling with activity. You are my love and hope. I LOVE YOU.

Letter II

Lady of love and hope, my dear wife! I write to you with a heart so filled with the ardor of your love that it cannot be contained by this confining world. I greet you with the same heart and my heart takes wing like a bird, to nestle in our love-nest, where every corner emits the eternal scent of your love. By the time this letter reaches you, the first two years of my sentence will have elapsed like a sigh in the wind.[16] Even if I had to wait two centuries, my heart would still be beating with the joy and hope of hearing your soothing voice, conversing with the flowers and birds of our house. And I miss my dear Mamani so much that—every moment—I want to put my forehead to the prayer rug of her kind heart and recite with tears the prayer of love. I know that our day is not too distant. I LOVE YOU.

---

16 Houshang was sentenced to 15 years in prison.

FROM HOME

My Houshang, man of my home, my companion, my love, I greet you! My birthday, too, came to pass. A year was added to the years of being with you, and our love has ripened further. And with every test of love, humans get closer to their essence, which is the eternal union with light—bees with flowers, moths with flames—and the tower of love. Today, I see myself in you and you in me. And, in the garden of our eternal love, all our pains of separation, our broken hearts, our sorrows that weigh so heavy on our hearts, and the bruises that grate our spirits, will come to pass, and hope will stand tall. Darling, this is the sound of the heartbeat of the earth. It has been there since time immemorial and shall remain until eternity. And you will return to the house, our little house whose every brick you know, whose every flower pot knows you, whose little kitchen we have cleaned together countless times. You shall not feel as among strangers. I am also alive with the hope of that day: to be with you, albeit I have never been without you. But the hope of being with you, of walking the streets with you, is something else. This is not too far down the road. Through the power of hope, it is as close as tomorrow. You know very well how much Mamani loves you.

Letter III

FROM PRISON
Hello lady of lovebirds. You left like a bird in the sunset sky. I saw you leave. You took wing and were lost in the gray evening. By Allah, how we have been separated! Did you ever think that a day would come when you would be going on a trip and I would stay behind bars dreaming of flight? I hope only for tomorrow. Nevertheless, you did good going on this journey, my lovebird. My beautiful songbird, make every use of your freedom. Fly as much as you can in the infinite sky. You can't imagine how painful it is for someone to be left only with the memory of flight. Today is Thursday and exactly a week has passed since we last met. But it seems that a century has elapsed. Mashhad is not too far from me but appears to be light years away.[17] I was eagerly awaiting our next meeting behind the glass pane. I was not fortunate to behold your eyes. My heart missed a beat. I knew you wouldn't come. I am restless, a little under the weather. I am hollow inside and all of this is a symptom of love. From behind bars I imagine your gaze and hope fills my heart. Love *exists* as long as you *do* and hope *exists* as long as you *do*. I breathe in this hope until we can fly together. I love you as much as the birds, as much as flight itself. Kiss Mamani all over her face. I LOVE YOU. I LOVE YOU. I LOVE YOU.

---

17 We used the Northeastern city of Mashhad to refer to Germany.

My Houshang, my caged bird, I love you. I know you and know that your wings will not forget how to fly and the agony of waiting for the moment to take flight will come to an end. Darling, I have repeatedly stressed that as long as there is hope, everything will be alright. Life is the arena for the power of hope to be tested. If this hope is alive in you and if it is grafted into your body, it will overcome most sadnesses, even sicknesses. You are not the only person going through difficulties, nor am I the luckiest woman on earth, but I am happy as long as I know that you are well. In a sense, I am also behind bars when I enviously look at couples that walk hand in hand. I have thousands of preoccupations—the condition that you are in, paying the bills, taking care of Mamani, and being careful not to lose the job that I have, speaking in the place of cockroaches and mice,[18]

---

18 For a few months after the arrest of Houshang, I decided to keep away from home, staying with different friends, lest the security forces would also come after me. With time, when it became clear that all those that were supposed to be arrested were already in jail—and tired of this drifting lifestyle—I returned home. Returning home, however, was the beginning of another set of challenges. I was without both job and money. It was then that I decided to go back to dubbing for TV-shows. But the work environment had changed, mirroring the situation elsewhere. We had sold our phone landline to go on a trip to Greece some years back and we had been unable to purchase another as there was a long waiting list. At the time, in the midst of the Iran-Iraq War, the country was marred by great shortages. I had to go to a public phone every day and call the person whose job it was to assign the dubbing works. On most days, he didn't have anything to offer. That was the most difficult period in my life. Adapting to the new Islamicized, moralizing, sanctimonious atmosphere wrenched my heart. At times this made me excitable and over-sensitive, as this letter clearly shows. These were the days when my dubbing job

because this is our main source of income, and then we should go to Mashhad, because we are indebted to one of our relatives there. Despite all this, I am standing tall. I am hopeful and in love. I also want you not to lose heart, to keep your spirits up, in the hope of your impending release. I love you deeply.

---

would force me to dub for mice and cockroaches. Later, when I mentioned this very fact in Kaveh Golestan's film *Sabt-e Haqiqat* [Documenting Reality] I ran into trouble with the authorities. In that documentary, the famous Iranian photographer, journalist, and filmmaker interviews several journalists on the Revolution of 1979 and how their lives have changed thereafter. I mentioned how I had been to Neauphle-le-Château in France when Ayatollah Khomeini was there and that I then interviewed the spiritual leader in his exile. I also mentioned that I was barred from practicing journalism following the Revolution and that I had to do dubbing to make ends meet. Golestan subsequently asked me what my work entailed and I explained that I spoke for cockroaches and mice (alluding to the cartoon characters). Hardliners, especially those who ran the newspaper *Keyhan*, took this reference to be an innuendo on those in power. It is noteworthy that the deputy of the Minister of Guidance admonished me years later for my figurative use of cockroaches and mice. "It was a barbed comment you made," he said.

Letter IV

We both have plenty of unknown psychological corners and this is no cause for bewilderment. I see the world from my own corner. I am happy with the thought of union with the beloved; at the same time, without the beloved Hell and Paradise are all the same to me. Kindness can only be found where the beloved resides. I want you to feel the same, and this is my blind spot. Houshang, you self-centered lover, so you want everything for yourself? What about her? In this constricted environment, you have come to a new understanding of her and discovered a new meaning in the fragrant book of her mind. You have found her feminine virtue, a virtue akin to that of saints, the virtue of an Eastern woman. This love is larger than the love of myself and it makes me proud of you. Once in my life I did not go astray and that was when I looked for love in you. Once I made a mistake and that was to make me the object of your love. In the trenches of the battlefield of your love, I have been empowered to not go astray—and because I have drawn you to the frightful whirlpool of my life, I have fouled up. All your bruises come from me, causing so much pain and suffering. You admonish me because you think that I am not considering what is going on in your life? My lovely mermaid, you deserve the happiest moments life has to offer and I have no gifts for you except misery and pain. Forgive me and know that the most real and powerful hope in this world seethe in my heart. If I share my sadness with you, it is because

I have no one else to share it with. I love you as much as love itself.

Darling, my Houshang! I love you. The confines of
your prison cell suffocate me in body and soul, and your
hopeful melancholy resides in me as well. I also feel
stifled. I become short of breath. Every time I hear of
someone's release from the prison, I see your accompa-
nying gaze. But my darling, at this point, you and I are
placed in a situation that dictates patience. We need a
kind of patience that will empower us without wearing
us down. We will again walk the streets hand in hand
and slack our thirst in the bottomless well of our love.
This much is certain to me, and the price we need to
pay is the effort of making these difficult days pass with
ease. Darling, when you speak of mistakes and going
astray, when you talk about the "frightful whirlpool"
of your life—my heart skips a beat. Have I ever complained about our life? Have I disclaimed it or shown
that I don't deserve it? How do you allow yourself to
separate my life from yours and then look at it though
our common view only? Yes, we have suffered plenty,
but we have also had many joyous moments. We have
lived fully in the wholesomeness of our love. I wouldn't
trade a single second of my life, even in moments of
pain, for the world. Our life has not ended, and even if
I had only one day to live, that day would last as long
as the years of our separation. On that day, we shall live
eternally, not unlike when I can pay a visit to you. When
I see you, even for a few minutes, I see, hear, and feel
you for days to come. My husband, always remember

that love can only be appreciated by those who have grasped its value. Don't envy the happiness of those who have not paid the price for their love. That kind of happiness is akin to having seen photographs only of a lotus, or regarded the early morning dew only as a drop of water. Darling, my love, we shall overcome these hurdles, provided that you never separate yourself from me. Don't forget that our hopes and sorrows are one, and the both of us are one. Mamani loves you as well.

Letter V

FROM PRISON

Hello my lotus lady.[19] Suddenly it is drizzling: A vernal morning in the midst of summer. It is the almost inaudible song of hope in the midst of the loneliness of the desert. Flowers and plants become moist. Sparrows shake their feathers. I remember you coming out of the water, trembling like a little sparrow. Four o'clock and the flowers are drenched in dew. When I kiss the white four-o'clock, water drops fall to the ground like tears rolling down your cheeks. In the feast of lotuses, there are plenty of shed dews. The velvety, purplish lotus that with courage raises her eyes to the sky is soaked in dew. I look at her. Her many bristles are bristling. I get a whiff of her, I drink from the sap, and I eat the flower. Over my head clouds are roaming in the blue sky. A breeze is blowing, and, suddenly, the sun rises in the horizon. A flower blooms like hope. My heart is about to burst. My body is shaking with excitement. The earth is shaking from the reverberations of morning hope. It is drizzling. Today will also pass. You will

---

19 The lotus was our favorite flower. The two of us would compete over who could bring the news of a new bud gone into bloom. *The Lotus Lady* became the title of a novel that Houshang wrote in Gohar-Dasht Prison and handed to me during a visit—and I slipped it out of there. Autobiographical in nature, the book tells the story of a couple whose lives are transformed after the Revolution. Initially the woman is fragile as a flower but ultimately becomes tough as a nail. Using my name as the author, we later on sold the script to someone who expressed a desire to turn it into a film. It never got realized and I am not sure where the script is today. However, the money that we got for it back in 1989 really saved the day.

rain on me like a blessing and rise in me like the morning sun. You sing the song of hope. I fall in love again, like a young buck, in this vernal summer morning.

My companion, my Houshang! I don't know how much the world has seen of rain and how many flowers and plants that have grown on this earth. How many birds have flown in the sky since it all began? And I say this loudly: "I love you as much as all the rains, flowers, birds, and butterflies." My love, my heart palpitates to the bristling of yours, to the excitement of your body, and I bow to the expression of hope and humanity in you, to your faith in hope and humanity. My husband, I know that our innocent hopes, yours and mine, will eventually tear down these walls, will overcome these distances—between Tehran and Qezel-Hesar or between home and Evin—and you will return home under a canopy of the lotuses from your dream. Every morning you will count the colorful lotuses of our small flowerbox, and every evening you will hold a feast of love. Darling, the number of years is not important, what *is* important is how much we live in a year. And we have lived, we live, and we shall live fully, with the help of love and hope. Our love is titanic and our hope is robust. Mamani loves you too.

Letter VI

My love, my lady, with your every tear my soul is set on fire and I bloom with your every smile.[20] You have lived with anger and pain. You have pounded your tiny fist at the cold stone. You know how I sat without saying a word. I couldn't bring myself to say anything. What made me devastated and made breathing difficult was seeing your pain. You know that I sense your every breath and I behold your every gaze. Every tear of yours speaks to me of the suffering that you are enduring. The delicate flower-stem of your body is shaking with pain, and your big and compassionate heart is the reason you are able to endure all this pressure. But your tears are not all that emanates from your body. On a daily basis these glass panes witness a carousal of tears on both sides. But it is the rainbow of your smile that appears at the far side of these tears and gives me hope and joy. To be honest, right now, I am hopping mad. I wish you were on the other side of the window and could slit my throat to relieve your anger. But I will recite the poem that you composed! "Bring my fair beloved to me, and I know that my desire will return and burn to cinders in this yearning." As such, I take refuge in the radiating heat of your smile. I will overcome this pain and my green fingers will cultivate the happiness of tomorrow

---

20 My tears came when my struggles to keep hope alive in Houshang didn't bear fruit. Of course, in those days, I couldn't know what he was going through in prison, but I wanted him not to lose faith and hope.

from the soil of the hopelessness of today. I roar again: "My lady! Filled with hope, I pledge that my vernal heart will forever beat with faith and joy, awaiting union, and I will guard the honor of love."

Greetings good sir! I greet the one who is overcoming these chapters of pain. You *will* win over pain and, despite the agonies that the path brings, *will* bring home the sacred trophy of adversity overcome. Darling, my husband, I am elated that holding the torch of hope you have come out of the caldron of human existential agonies. Don't forget that life is an ocean and to know how to glide on its waves is the essence of existence, while hopelessness and despair are dark passages that can easily engulf you in darkness, keeping you from light and life. In this expression of rebirth, liberation as such will be yours and freedom will await you. My Houshang, I will also walk with you to the dawn of blossoms and go to the banquet of lotuses, water, and mirrors. Neither you nor I are alone. Loneliness cannot impose itself on us because we have each other. My wish is for our bond, which is stronger in these years of prison and of waiting behind prison doors, to take us to the future, a happier future. My love! tomorrow is not too distant. I LOVE YOU. So does Mamani.

Letter VII

FROM PRISON

My heavenly lady, my big blue! I call on you in the silence of the evening. I call on you with all my heart. My voice swirls in the clear blue sky, under the rays of the autumnal sun, and echoes against the backdrop of mountains topped with snow. I suddenly see an unknown bird cut through the horizon and she calls on me with her loving ululation. This is you, my bird of love and hope, coming from the clear blue sky to let your smile make all pain go away. Another autumn passes and a new winter comes. This is the fifth winter of separation and I know that no autumn or winter can harm the budding plant of our love and hope. I thus smile and extend my arms to hold your arms across the distance and to pick buds from your eyes. Kiss Mamani all over her face.

My dear Houshang! You are the companion of my moments and the hope of my life. I greet you with all my heart. I love you in your transparency. My love, another winter is also coming to pass, but love birds will tweet again when winter icicles begin to melt. Again, the beautiful stream of life starts to flow. Hope is radiating and we believe in life again. Our love is based on such faith in existence. Yes, as long as this faith and that hope exist, blossoms will come forth again. Then smile. From the bottom of your heart, smile at life and its beauties, its sufferings, which we shall overcome. Mamani also loves you.

Letter VIII

FROM PRISON

Grand lady of my love, you are the spring season showing up in the middle of my winter. I greet you like the scent of renewal. In the coldest winter of our separation, we again return to the vernal flowerage of our marriage. This was the day when you descended to earth like a white bird, and brought flowers and merriment to our house. You gave me your kind hand. I looked you in the eyes and through their starry radiance all darkness was made trifle and all pain immaterial. Nine years have elapsed since then and all our seasons have been the spring. You mentioned how Uncle[21] on that day let his tears roll down, perhaps foreshadowing all the nights we will have to keep memories alive through tears. The starriest nights of the universe bring me from the Milky Way to the eternity of your love. My virtuous lady, even flowers envy your chastity. May the anniversary of our love always be kept alive! Drown my dear Mamani in kisses, and I mean drown. I kiss and one-up you.[22]

---

21 Refers to our executed friend Rahman Hatefi.
22 The issue of one-upping each other has a story behind it. To this day we look for new ways to surprise each other on occasions such as anniversaries or birthdays. We try to come up with the least expected gifts, or unexpected presentations. This was also the case during Houshang's prison term. For instance, in one of our anniversaries, the wife of another prisoner whose day of visit coincided with mine came by the house. Over the speaker she asked me to come down forthwith as she had something important to tell me. I ran downstairs to open the door and I came face to face with a large bouquet of flowers Houshang had arranged to be delivered to our door. On numerous occasions I did similar things to surprise him. We called this "one-upping" each other. When we were one-upped by life itself we had to appeal to these ruses to challenge it.

Hello, my Houshang. You spoke of our love and the years of our communion, of our tears, of winters of separation, and of the coming spring. My love, I want you to know that the green garden of love is boundless. That garden houses things much grander than happiness and sadness, things as immense as love, things that cannot be circumscribed by words, but appear in the most practical moments of life, an appearance that gives impressions. Life is the ground for manifestations of love, and this is something amazing. Sir! Last night I dreamt of a man who was wearing a green dress and had his face covered; only the grandeur remained of him and he kissed my cheeks with his heart. And Mamani said: "Lucky you." And I said: "Lucky all of us, this love is joy itself."

Letter IX

FROM PRISON

Hello my lady of forever, grand lady of my love, hello. By the time you receive this letter, your old man is almost 37. Where along this path will I hold your hands again? No matter when, I will live, look at the sky, listen to the birds for that moment. Isn't it silly, my grand lady, that your old man still harbors such sensations? "When passions of old age soar…"[23] I am learning many new dishes. Last night I learned how to make broiled cheese or, as Azita the numskull calls it, "cheesebroil".[24] I made it with such love and I ate it in solitude. I wish you were next to me instead of all the others that I share this space with. Each meal would be meaningful only if you took part in it. But I know that I will return one day and make you all the delicious dishes that I have learned. My hopeful arms are open. I love you as much as Time. Drown Mamani in kisses.

---

23 Refers to a Persian expression that in complete translation reads: "When passions of old age soar / In tandem dishonor may roar."
24 Azita was a friend notorious for her cooking. We joked that she even burned boiled eggs.

Hi darling, my love. Happy birthday to you! Even if you reach 370, we will hold hands on a day of love. My love, it is good that you are learning how to cook, because I have forgotten even the green-bean rice and the chicken dishes that I knew. Either the rice turns out salty or the chicken will burn. Naturally, it is the fault of all the chickens and rice in the world. Really, look at it this way, when you come back, chickens and rice will be the same again; however, since my talent for cooking, or keeping house for that matter, is next to nil, then it would be ideal to have a husband who knows how to broil cheese; otherwise, I would have to blame the chickens for burning. Darling, I love your heart. I am safekeeping your tears in my heart, patient and hopeful, until that tomorrow when you come back home and I shall rain with tears. Mamani loves you too.

Letter X

In my spring and my New Year, my lady, I greet you. Again Nowruz is upon us and the spring must come and flowers must bloom.[25] The year renews itself and my pain and hope also renew themselves. Yearning fills me. Yet another spring spent away from you cannot be spring. Hope brings youth to my heart, however, for as long as you exist, spring will be there. If blossoms, rain, scents, birds and humanity have any significance it is because of you. And again, life will be born in your eyes. Therefore, my love, may spring smile at you. May all your days be like days of spring! Drown Mamani in kisses and wish her a happy New Year. Smile at the flowers in our tiny garden and ask the nightingales to compose our symphony of tomorrow.

---

25 To me, this particular time of the year was exceptionally stressful, as I had to keep my job as well as go to see Houshang whenever possible. And this was always a busy time of long lines at the prison waiting room. Late winter days were often snowy and icy, especially on the way to Karaj (and Qezel-Hesar Prison). It was on one of those visits that I woke up at 4 am and pleaded with my car: "Be kind to me today, because it is a delicate and difficult day." The road to Karaj, however, was icy and mine was among the first cars braving the conditions. At some point, my car skidded, gyrated twice and got caught "between bars" in the middle of the highway. I was afraid of coming out of my car in the darkness but neither could I be sitting there. After several attempts to break the car free, I slammed on the dashboard, tired and frustrated. "You are such a traitor," I told my car and let my head rest on the wheels to cry. I was in that position for ten minutes. Without expecting much, I tried the break and gas pedal again. This time, to my bewilderment, the car slid out with ease. It was a good car, a true friend. It understood me and knew that I must be the first person to show up at the prison gates so that I can be the first one to leave the visiting room. I reached the television building, where I did the dubbing, just in time.

Hello my husband, my companion! Indeed, renewal is the inevitable fate of these years as well as their pains and hopes. This year, however, is the fifth New Year without you. I can only wish that this one may bring us the ability to smile in the face of fear and to realize some hope in the face of despair. May this be the year of blossoms, rain, scents, and flowers in the house! May this be a year when you wake me up every day by announcing the budding of a new flower in our little garden! May this be a year when freedom can be part of our fate! Let love, the flowers that I have planted, the nightingale that have nestled in our poplar tree, and the doves that rest on our window ledge, along with Mamani and I, wish you a happy spring!

Letter XI

Hello, lady of spring. You exhale and the flowers bloom. You smile and the grass begins to grow. You stroll and mountain springs spout underfoot, swallows greet you high above. We are those two flowers that open up in a tender garden of love.[26] Until that day I send you florets of love from the four seasons of my heart, which is full of vernal hopes. I yearn for you the way a mountain spring does for the sea. I greet you with the scent of all the flowers in the world. For as long as you exist, lady of spring, the garden of our lives shall be vernal. I love you as much as all the vernal buds.

---

26 Some people are not made for handiworks—but the prison environment gives inmates time to learn previously unimaginable skills. Houshang learned to carve birds and flowers out of wood. He also learned to polish ordinary coins to the point that they would reflect the transparency of love.

Beyond Distances
Letters of 1366
[April 1987-March 1988]

Nooshabeh Amiri & Houshang Asadi

Letter I

FROM PRISON
My lady of spring, I salute your person and your day of birth. I salute you. You bloom under the sun, multiply beauty in a mirror, and bring color to life. My lady, in this season of your birth, I have a new lease on life. You are the melodious spring symphony that hangs in the air and whose presence causes flowers to bloom and birds to sing. How can I explain the happiness that envelops me this spring? For, as long as you exist, as long as your smile beams, your tears roll, your kindness spreads, and your wrath lashes, the autumn of my heart turns endlessly into spring. Lady of the sun and the mirror and the swallows, happy is your day of birth. My heart beats for the day I hold your hands beyond distances and can place the most beautiful flowers of the world in your hair. Give my kind Mamani a shower of kisses.

My man of every season, greetings to you. Though a wall temporarily separates you from them, you belong to all the seasons. You go beyond these walls to connect to seasons and you compose the sweet symphony of life. Human beings are nothing without the power to remember seasonal changes beyond confining walls and glass panes. Darling, I live for the day when you come back, and for us to renew this power together. And I strongly wish that this power will never leave us. We will always have the marks that suffering have left on body and soul, but all sufferings potentially strengthen the human dignity. The mettle of a love is tested through hardships. Our love has survived these years of prison and pain. I LOVE YOU.

Letter II

I greet you lady of hope and love and lotuses. I start with admitting to having done you wrong. I beseech kindness—instead of rage—from your eyes. I beseech amity—instead of enmity—from your voice. I continue this letter by repeating that I have done you wrong. I repeat the power of love and the faith in love that your gaze evokes, as nothing will have the power to crush my faith in you and my faith in love. I carry on with admitting to having done you wrong. I submerge myself in the euphoria of reading every line of your letters. My whole life is impregnated with hope and love out of this euphoria. I proceed with admitting to having done you wrong. I am proud of you. You have transformed yourself from that tearful girl that I knew to the thoughtful, robust, and proud lady that you now are.[27] You have leaped so far ahead of me that I fear in this race I will not be able to catch up with you. Yours is the dream of

---

27 I was born in a feminine environment. In the absence of a father and under the guidance of a mother whose heart was lucid, the life of my sister and I was full of promises of an utopian future. But life had different plans for us. My sister passed away at the age of 20. She had a heart condition and died after a long surgery. And I, who was known as the "Orange-juice reporter" (because my mother famously insisted that her children should drink a glass of fresh orange juice every day and take vitamin supplements) was thrown into the turbulent sea of revolution. Some friends would say: "Nooshabeh is like a flower whose petals fall with the slightest breeze." Hence I was surprised by the petals that wouldn't fall in the wind.

Back then and even today I tell my friends: "Human beings have great potentials that will appear in times of difficulty." Houshang wrote the script for *The Lotus Lady* based on those capacities.

conquering the seven-domed heavens. I love you and I end this letter by admitting to having done you wrong.

I greet you my good man, my kind man. I shall start with hope again. And this: Hope is conviction, faith, and not a figment of imagination. Hope is health and not a cure. Hope is a life force and not the force of clinging to life. Life is of a different texture than the imagination. I say these things—for you to know that the "race" you spoke of is taking place within the domains of hope, and it is in these domains that life, love, and reason are tested. If hope is true, if it is a part of us, if it is *us*, then our body and soul will remain healthy; if we prescribe a cure other than hope, we will be deprived of health. Life seems to be the ground where hope is put to test, and nothing more. And having patience along the path of hope is the most beautiful of qualities. Let us thus hope for the day we can continue our life together in our house.

Letter III

My dear nun, I greet you.[28] I will start with I LOVE YOU. I summon your name along with the flowers. I await the sound of your voice. I learn how to cook. I sigh from the memory of our little veranda; I cook Mirza-Qasemi,[29] put it on our spread, and in my imagination call on you to come. In my imagination I walk by your side in streets and gardens. I gaze at the sky and imagine you in the passing of birds. And I am apprehensive that our forced separation, which will soon outlast our shared life, will affect our minds to such an extent that we are going to be unable to understand each other. I may remain that playful child and you a nun. I push the apprehensions aside and my hope dawns. I kiss Mamani and end with I LOVE YOU.

---

28 On one of the visits Houshang asked me to open my veil a little bit so that he could peek at my naked body. I was so furious at this suggestion that he was shocked. We had not understood one another. I felt so alienated in that heavy, guilt-ridden environment that I would even cover my face if I could. The walls and doors of that space were alien and insecure to me. This puritanical attitude was partially due to my upbringing, but mostly because of the prison atmosphere. There was (and still is) a room set aside for married couples, called "the religiously-sanctioned room". A prisoner could potentially spend the night together with his spouse in that room. But the way guards would look at women who accompanied their men to these rooms made me cringe. Also, prison officials often tried to convince us that because our men had acted against the Islamic Republic, they were religiously impure.

29 A dish from the Northwestern Caspian Region of Iran, made with barbecued eggplants, tomatoes, eggs, garlic, and oil.

FROM HOME

My Houshang, my whimsical man, I greet you. I start with conviction, faith in love. I repeat your name with the solidity of life and await the sound of your voice with the conviction of love. I work, I don't; I have money, I don't; I am sad, I am not; I suffer, I don't, and I call you and I call on your faith in love and the power of love. And I am apprehensive that you may forget this power under the weight of those walls and words, may forget that we have lived together for years and that it is only for a short while that glass panes and walls—which are nothing in comparison to the power of love—have imposed themselves on us. And do remember that the memory of lovers have always remained alive while no one even bothers to take their picture next to prison bars and walls. Yes, push apprehension aside. Have faith in me and in my faith in this faith.

Letter IV

My dear Houshang, man of my home! I greet you with the love that flows in the world. With this I become a sky that awaits a bird like you. My love, the rest of your term will pass as if it was a simple nightmare and we will come together in daylight. If you look at it closely, you will see that the entire hubbub of the world orbits around this source of light. Mamani also says hello. She misses you and your presence around the house. She has her hands raised to the heavens, praying and anxiously waiting. I told her as well that these days will come to an end and again we will have bustle in the house. Darling, take care of yourself and your hope until that day; know that a true lover sees both union and separation as signs of love. I LOVE YOU.

Letter V

FROM PRISON

My lady, sky of my hope, I greet you! I salute the bird that wants to be worthy of the blue sky of your love and hope. In the fifth autumn of separation, this bird flaps its wings of hope with all his strength so that I can fly in the loving expanse of that sky. My lady, I take heart in this autumnal wind and know that no autumn can affect the ever-green garden of our love. To the contrary, it is the power of our love that confronts all the autumns of despair. In that manner we will ride the autumn till we reach spring, and the eternal leaves of our love will sing in the alleys and streets of this city. I salute my dear Mamani. I can only tolerate being away from her by hoping that this separation will be temporary. I LOVE YOU.

FROM HOME

My dear man, my love, it was said to be a "visit" but it ended as soon as it started.[30] I wasn't even suspecting when I heard a voice asking us to say our farewells. Now with the memory of that short visit I can live for hours, and I graft this memory into the hope of realizing our eternal union. Yes my love, it is as such I am also grappling with suffering and sadness, to continue only with hope. Now that the autumn is flapping its wings against my window, I think of a spring when I would eventually open my windows, and once again we shall hear the sound of birds. My Houshang, my precious, the sadness of today will cast its shadow on our lives for ever, but the ensuing roots of our happiness will be just as strong, without anyone being able to understand its depth. I LOVE YOU.

---

30 We never got to know when—and on the basis of which procedures—prison officials decided to grant us visits. Nor did we know beforehand if our names actually would be called out and our wish for a visit would be granted. Some visits took place right in the visiting room. They forced prisoners to sit on a soiled blanket before letting family members in. I still remember the sound of children who called their fathers. We would sit across from the prisoner on the blanket while the numerous guards would pace up and down the hall. We still had moments to exchange news and to receive the handmade articles of prisoners—necklaces made with dried bread dough, or dried flowers on a cardboard, etc. It was on one of these visits, Houshang gave me a stack of papers that he had hidden underneath his dress. I shoved it inside my veil. For the rest of the visit I was anxious. When they announced that the time was up and I began to leave, it was as if I had dynamite taped to my body. It was only after reaching the car that I pulled out the manuscript: *The Lotus Lady*.

Letter VI

Eminent lady, Mrs. Hamideh Amiri, a.k.a. Lady Doctor,[31] with due respect, I hereby inform you, lady, that your husband (Mr. Asadi) has decided to terminate his association with you and is entering into matrimony with a beautiful, fat woman whose nose is smaller and whose feet are straighter that yours. She is not as obstinate as you and follows orders to the letter. Therefore, with utmost relief, and to make sure, I request the dissolution of our marriage. Kindly regard this letter as a formal petition for divorce and appear before the nearest court in order for the formal procedures to begin. You are warned that no excuse—official holiday or some similar justification—shall be accepted. Sorry, I am an assclown.

---

31 Hamideh is my given name. Lady Doctor refers to me at that time applying to the PhD program in the School of Sociology. Houshang became elated and started calling me Lady Doctor from that day on. On the day of the entrance examination, when I came into the large hall of the university, I realized that most of those taking the exam were higher government officials. I immediately left the premises. Since then I have tried four times to get my PhD and each time I have failed. Today, I am a student at the University of Leiden. Going to school is, to me, a way to deal with the difficulties of life.

Dear Mr. Houshang the Great, a.k.a. Sikhka,[32] with due respect, I hereby inform you, respectable sir, that your wife (the one writing this letter) has decided, and to make sure, not to follow your orders, and thereby with utmost relief refuses to acknowledge the aforementioned request by insisting: You are a part of my life and I am not mad enough to separate you from myself as it would mean death to me. And you know that when it comes to madness, I am mad only about love, and it is through this madness that I have reached wisdom,

---

32 My husband and I were students at the same university department—School of Communication Studies. The warm and passionate atmosphere there supported the livelihood of many. We formed lasting associations, memorable friendships, engaged in passionate student debates; and honored the Student Day of Azar 16 (the month of Azar here coincides with December), which was the date of three students being killed on campus in 1953 after demonstrations protesting the presence of then Vice President Richard Nixon.

The boys were all playful. Girls like me, who had just finished high school, were shy and punctual. The boys joked around a lot, but we couldn't understand what they were getting at. No one was more out of the loop than I. Because of this, others called me Mikh, meaning straight (as a "nail"). I knew what it meant to be called a nail. Looking like a dork and not getting them at all. Thus, "Nail" became my pseudonym. Later it changed to Mikhi and then Mikhka. I called Houshang Sikhka as a tender diminutive of "Sikh", in the meaning of having strict behavior. I also called Houshang Hushka. Having read *The Death of Ivan Ilyich* by Leo Tolstoy, our names changed to Nooshkin and Hushkin. These were not nom de guerre but whimsical names that we used as terms of endearment. The heroes of *The Death of Ivan Ilyich* were also a couple who were separated by a revolution. And one spent time in jail. It is true that books get their fodder from naïve individuals like us. We reinvented ourselves through the book and wore the hero's dress only to make life easier.

although wisdom holds many definitions, as does madness. But based on our shared history I have reached a definition of love, whereby its absence is to be regarded as madness. I LOVE YOU.

Letter VIIa

FROM PRISON

My beautiful former wife, please accept my lukewarm greetings. In the previous letter I promised to introduce the person that I have fallen in love with, so that you may get to know her. Therefore, I hereby inform you, respectable lady, who used to be my wife, that springtime descends in the glittering of my new love's eyes, she has a smile on her lips that makes flowers bloom, from her teeth rays emanate to break into dawn, her tears are meteorite showers of the night of love, her voice impregnates the soil of wheat fields, her every breath comes from love. This makes whiteness, darkness, fatness, thinness, tallness and shortness all to become meaningless. You have, no doubt, guessed who my new love is. It is your own esteemed self. Thus, following the previous petition for divorce, I ask for your hand again. Are you in agreement with this?

Letter VIIb

FROM PRISON[33]

Dear Mrs. Hamideh Amiri, my former wife, with due respect, I again inform you, obstinate Mikhka, that, as you can see from the subject of this letter (fear nothing), your divorce from me is a foregone conclusion. Your dilly-dallying will not solve a thing. It is necessary to hereby inform you that I (meaning myself) have fallen in love. My object of love has characteristics different from yours. She is white and not like you—a cockroach. She is not as obstinate and follows my commands to the letter. In addition, rather than shrinking on a daily basis, she is gaining weight.[34] In future letters I will introduce her to you. Kindly give my regards to my former mother-in-law. I love you both.

---

33 By this made up divorce episode Houshang was able to send two letters in one month.
34 In those years I would get thinner and thinner. This was more obvious under the black veil that we had to wear to go for visits.

Letter VIII

FROM PRISON

Greetings my wise lady, I am not sure which starry night I should proffer you—that would be deserving of your thoughtful and pure love. In these days, when another year of my life goes the way of winter, and your old man turns 38, I see myself as a small child that requires your love and smile more than ever. This is a child whose heart beats in yearning for you and is constantly apprehensive of deserving your love. My beautiful and wise lady, the old man that greeted you from the beginning of the world, will be a pupil of love, wisdom and patience in the portico of your smile. Can you hear the cries of this beginner's heart?

My kind man, my intimate, hello. I like you to know that even at 380, your life will not go the way of winter; your life and our life are rays of love and love knows of no winter. Love is the loudest expression of life. When you come upon it, there is only one way ahead of you, and that is the way of spring. What ears desire but do not hear the sound of spring in discovering the power of love? Darling, we are now among the audience of spring and the discoverers of love, and this is a blessing granted to us. Even at 38, I wish your beginner's heart the energy of spring and the power of love. I love your heart.

Letter IX

My beautiful and wise lady, my love, my soul mate! I greet you with my solar heart so that the sixth winter of our separation can turn into springtime. My lotus lady, the month of Bahman is the month of our marriage and separation.[35] This is a month in which our loving hearts were forever united. It is also the month when we were separated and separation showed us the grandeur of love, to which nothing under the heavens compares. It is in this separation I come closer to you and sing the song of love. Our eternal bond becomes stronger in my heart. My beautiful and wise love, on the eleventh anniversary of our blissful union, I will live with the hope that the winter of separation can soon become the spring of reunion. I kiss your eyes and proffer you my true love. Even if eleven centuries pass, my heart shall beat with the reverberation of your name. Kiss dear Mamani. I LOVE YOU.

---

35 These dates in the month of Bahman of the Persian calendar coincides with February.

FROM HOME

Man of my home, my kind soul, I greet you. And again, I say yes. Yes to the eleventh anniversary of the coming together of our hearts. I wish now that I on that day had screamed YES the first time that I was asked.[36] To make up for it, let us have another ceremony when you are back. I will say "yes" even before the go-between has read the formula to fulfill the marriage. Others will laugh at me and our true-love hearts will be submerged in merriment. I will get into fights with you again and you will have to make up with me, even if you are in the right. You are to make up first, because you know that I won't feel relieved unless you make up with me. I miss all the days of being with you. I yearn for days that the winter of separation can turn into a gusty spring of union. I love you as much as my dreams.

---

36 It is customary in Iran for the bride not to accept to take the vow when asked by the prelate, until the request has been repeated three times.

Letter X

My wife, my kind love, I salute you. I salute the one in whose eyes I become young again. The earth celebrates your day of birth by coming alive in the redolence of your breath. My wise lady, when the year renews itself, go to our little portico and see that my heart is like a bird sitting in our tall poplar tree, congratulating you on the arrival of another spring season. This bird, whose voice has the sound of spring, sings: Our eternal spring-time is closer than ever. I, the owner of that heart, will come one day soon to stroll eternally with you in the florid gardens of love. Let this happen. Even if you get into fights with me until the end of the earth, I will turn your wrath into laughter with a kiss. Wish Mamani a happy New Year and kiss her lavishly. She loves you as much as all spring seasons.

My Houshang, man of my home, hello! I greet your goodness. As long as you exist, springtime will come. I greet your vernal presence and your heart, which beats to the chirping of birds, the germination of plants, and whatever that carries being and becoming in itself. I greet the spring of your soul and the spring of your immaculate and humane dreams about life and the living. That is the living that befits humanity, the human being that you are, the human being that I love, the human being that extends the wings, not only in springtime but in fall and winter, to glide towards love, and who can only live in the fire of love. Let this fire never go out. Man of my home, I wish you, us, better New Year celebrations. I love you as much as spring. Mamani loves you too.

Autumnal Trails
Letters of 1367
[April 1988-January 1989]

Nooshabeh Amiri & Houshang Asadi

Letter I

FROM PRISON

Hello lady, my springtime lady! Your vernal birthday is just around the corner. Your birthday will come, wise lady of fountains of hope and love. The world and I will become new in your eyes. Your birthday will arrive and love will once again be born with your morning breath, redolent with the scent of blossoms and joyous with the song of rain. I will bloom like a flower to the tune of your voice—that always reverberates in me. I scream: I am the happiest man, the brightest star, the most tuneful songbird in this infinite universe. In my heart dawns the eyes that define the meaning of life, love, and spring. Lady, springtime, lady of all songbird songs, lady of all garden blossoms, at your feet I shall spread all the stars of heavens, to celebrate your birthday, which is also the birthday of existence and love. You are an eternal dawn; dawn on me!

FROM HOME

Sir! My dear sir, greetings! I open my eyes to the world. In the darkness I feel for light. Having found it, makes this a love that to me conjugates being. You *are* love and love *is* you. Thus I conjugate "being." With me, with my love, flowers of every spring sing the song of the victory of light over darkness. Even cacti bear flowers. Sparrows sing delicately alongside nightingales and springtime: love, hope, springtime, love, hope, springtime. Yes my love, every spring I recover you and repeat the being of love in you.

Letter II

FROM PRISON

Hello my exceptional mother![37] You have become so old that, notwithstanding the fact that I am your only child, I like to embrace you like the grandmother of fairy tales, and let the smell of your rose-scented hair clear my springtime melancholy. My dear mother! This aging means ripening and maturing. When the body is still on the borderlines of youth, there is a promise of miracles in the air. And this is the miracle of your precious existence, that allows many a weary heart to seek solace in you. For this I take pride in you, but I can hardly tolerate it, for I fear that it may be due to our separation and my idleness. But my precious mother, know that the child in me draws strength from your maternal wisdom, and overcomes the melancholy of separation until springtime of union comes.

---

37 As prison rules allowed only one letter a month, we went around it by writing to each other in the name of different people, in this case he addresses me as his mother.

Hello my exceptional son! You are so young that, not-withstanding the fact that you know you are my only child, you still utter words that only a one-and-only child would. Of course you are more mature than your peers. When you talk about your issues—you see clearly the process through which you arrive at your conclusions. My sweetheart, my son, what words can I employ to say that we must accept our predicament. And as soon as your love germinated within me, it gave meaning to our lives. This meaning can only be explained within this relationship. Thus, my one-and-only, know that the object of this love is unconditionally you, and it demands that you set aside any kind of paranoia or disillusionment about its origins. You don't know how much I love you, do you?

Letter III

FROM PRISON

My exceptional lady, my sweetheart! Is love jealous or is it that it in its evolution has to pass through jealousy?[38] Is this a natural process or is it a defect in me? I am not sure. Whatever it is, I have this jealousy. I have become this way. It is something that seethes within me. The mind tries to tether it but the heart screams it again. I brim with hatred, thinking that another name shall soil our amorous whispers, even if I have not had any indication of the existence of such a person. I know that I am over-reacting, but what can I do, my heart is passionately going through this newfound jealousy. Is it madness? If it isn't, then it is a part of the madness of love. Allow for it to be there. My lady, my wise lady whom I trust more than anything or anyone else in this world, perform a miracle with your words and cure the madness that has come to possess your lover. I LOVE YOU.

---

38 I wanted to appeal to a famous actor on behalf of Houshang but Houshang was against it. I failed to understand the reason. In this letter he explains that it was out of jealousy.

Hello my man, my exceptional man! Love is not jealous. Love wants to monopolize. But how much can it monopolize? This can only go along to the point where boundaries between two bonding individuals are still kept distinct. Besides, respecting these boundaries, true love, reasonable love, mature love also reserves spaces of solitude for the lovers. Those in love will feel the power of their love in the absence or presence of the beloved—even in the spaces of solitude. That solitude and those boundaries are, as such, complimentary. One needs the other. Without boundaries and without solitude there will be no love. In this sense, I desire you and want you all for myself, and I repeat your name in my moments of solitude. And I love you in this way. You have your own spaces of solitude, don't you? I LOVE YOU.

Letter IV

My delicate mother, my sweetheart! Greetings to you! You are my old wise lady, who becomes clearer as she ages. You shine like a sun on my soul. I am unable to say how very anxious my heart is to see you. I have thrived like a seedling in the palm of your virtuous love. From those hands I tasted the sweetness of a caress! From your warm bosom I drank the milk of compassion! This means that my existence draws its power from you and that my heart beats to the rhythm of your kind heart. Another season has passed and your hair, which is now turning white, is an indication of the years of separation. Lo how my heart has suffered from being away from you. I love you mother, my life.

My son, the light of my eyes! Hi, I hope you are well and in good spirits. It is good that you decided to write to your aging mother. I can't bear being apart from you. I know that you write mostly to your wife. She is no doubt blessed. I wonder to myself what that cockroach-legged creature possesses that has captivated my son to this extent. But then, humans need only a mat to sleep on and she is a good wife to you. My son, you should appreciate her because she has stood by your side and never complained. To be sure, she is very lucky! You are such a gem. I kiss your loving eyes. But my son, when you come back home, don't you just spend time with your wife. You have your brothers and sisters too, my son. Of course, you know all this but I am just saying. If all these years of separation have been hard on you, you can imagine what it has done to me. You are a part of my body. I await your arrival. Love you.

Letter V

FROM PRISON
Lady, kind lady, lady! Greetings! My fair lady, another autumn is on its way, and my heart, which is always turbulent like autumn, misses you as much as there are leaves falling to the ground. Do you see the children go to school? In their faces you can see your old man who, with his novice heart, is coming to your course to recite the lesson of love. Please don't remind me that I have been in your class for too long. I know, I know! But I still don't know its alphabet. I have not tasted a single drop of this ocean. I am a child whose heart beats with the excitement of coming to your class. I live with the hope of the day we can walk the streets of autumn, and all the leaves under our feet will become poems. I keep my heart warm with such hope and walk with you in its autumnal vicinity. Give my regards to dear Mamani. I LOVE YOU.

My Houshang, my man in prison! Greetings! I also resemble a schoolgirl unable to find her way into school. You are my school and providence has so decided that I be kept apart from, but madly wanting, this school. But our fate shall not remain the same. One day shall come when I will spend the whole day with you—and not just fifteen minutes. One day, you and I will review spring, autumn, winter and summer together. We will live fully in little time. On that day, I will not be far from the school of your love. On that day, you will feel like a student who have successfully completed all stages of his education and is now looking at a bright future. That day is not far away. I LOVE YOU.

Letter VI

My mother, my very life, my very youth! Greetings! I give my soul to you, mother. Your letter brought excitement, tears and smiles to me. Pity, though, that I sensed some sarcasm when you were talking about my wife. My lovely mother, you know that she, my wife, is not a "cockroach-legged creature." There is no one like her in this world. Nevertheless, you are right; I am too much under her sway. There is a limit to everything. She is not perfect. Look at her big nose! I did some thinking too, and I must admit that I have been less than attentive to my family. When I return, I will spend more time with my dear brother, my dearer father, and my dearest sister. If there will be any time left, I put it aside for her, my wife. If she decides to object, divorce would be the answer.

My son, my pumpkin, my moppet, my love bug, my joy! I kiss your beautiful face. I admire your perspicacity, your intelligence. I am so happy to learn of your health, both physical and mental. Your new attitude towards your wife clearly demonstrates this wholesomeness and the power of decision-making. Everyone knows that "women should be kept on a short leash;" besides, no one can replace the love that sisters and brothers lavish upon us. Truly, can your wife's love be compared to that of your kind and caring father, your dedicated sister, and your intelligent brother? And I am not even talking about myself here. Fate has dealt us these cards and we must play them. My dear son, the light of my eyes, I hope for the day you'll return home and make the proper choice—following my advice, of course— and keep your wife's ambitions at bay. What more can I say? Motherly love knows no boundaries.

Letter VII

My lady of love and hope, lady, lady of the sun! I wish I could find words that would describe my longing for you. How can I show my yearnings? You said that the best years of our lives had to be spent away from each other, that I had to approach the apex of 40 to discover that all things in this world are meaningless and empty without your love. It is in light of this late-found discovery that every day of being away from you appears like light years. I yearn to behold those eyes of yours, that burn to scream out the meaning of love and hope. I love you as much as all the stars and suns. I LOVE YOU, I love.

Houshang! Where are you my husband! I can't say my heart yearn for you because it has turned into ashes. I was with you twice a week for fifteen minutes. I have lived with that quarter of an hour. Now they have deprived me of those measly minutes.[39] And I can only

39 The frequency of visits during Houshang's prison term was highly irregular, depending on official policy or whim. The first year there where no visits at all, then once a month, then every other week, and for a while twice a week. If I were to say that the days we were deprived of visits were frightening, I have not said much to describe the horror. In the frightful summer of 1988 things were even worse than usual. We were deprived of our visits without any prior warning. In one of my previous visits, when I again begged the officials in prison to tell me something about my husband's fate, they just looked at me. I thought that they never paid attention to what I was saying. I thought that what reached their ears was not heard, or that they failed to comprehend what they heard. But this one had heard and understood everything. He just said one sentence: "Soon everything will be sorted out; those that are to go will go and those that are not will not." Based on what? What court? What law? What ruling? I didn't ask these questions. He had said his piece. My heart missed a beat. The following week, our visits were terminated for three months. How much suffering can a human being stand? We didn't receive any phone calls. Rumors and hearsay were flying around amongst the families of prisoners.

Finally, one day, the phone rang and a grainy voice said: "Come to Luna Park tomorrow!" The voice on the phone didn't even allow for a pause. Luna Park was a children's playground near Evin prison, but, surrealistically, the booth for prisoner information was also located in Luna Park. It was there that we had to form a queue and wait for the loudspeakers to call our names—to then board small buses and go to the main prison building on Evin Street for our visits. Needless to say, I didn't sleep that night. All night I walked up and down our little house. I imagined myself and the house without him. I imagined that I would set myself on fire in protest outside Luna Park or outside the Parliament. I saw before me that I was in flames but my body didn't burn. I saw that I was burning but that this had no effect on others. I saw that I was dying. Early in the morning, wrapped in the black veil, I was in Luna Park along with hundreds of people. Some cried, others shouted—but all were afraid. I was summoned to a tiny room. My body was shaking when I stepped

wonder why these days never come to pass so that I can walk into that room, to sit behind the glass, and drink from your words. Nevertheless, the experiences of the past few years have taught me that patience is medicine, a cure-all. These months will also come to pass and I will hang my lantern from your face, listen to the timbre of your voice, and will fall in love with a future where you will be in the house and the color of happiness will return to our walls. My Houshang, my husband, no one knows and can know how much I love you.

---

in. In that room they gave out numbers. You would take the number to an adjacent room, where they would tell you whether to reclaim the prisoner's belongings or go to meet him in another ward. No writing can do justice to what was going on inside of me in the space between these two rooms. My life was suspended in this space. My knees locked. I handed over the number I had been given. When I heard Houshang's ward location being announced, I was given a new lease on life. It was as if I had died and was born again. I was granted a visit. It was then it first occurred to me that I could cry.

It was only later that we learned what had actually taken place. In the summer of 1988 mass executions took place at Evin Prison. Some political prisoners where executed by shooting and others hung in the basement of the notorious prison. The bodies of executed prisoners were left at a cemetery on the southern outskirts of Tehran, called Khavaran. Khavaran was known as the cemetery for followers of the Baha'i Faith, who are considered impious. There are various statistics regarding the number of political prisoners executed that summer. Some estimates put it at 5,000. A selected number of families were able to identify their loved ones by birthmarks. Signs of mass graves have also been noted. The issue of these executions was never brought to the light of day in Iran and remains an open case outside of the country.

Letter VIII

FROM PRISON

Lady, my companion, my companion, my companion! Greetings! The strange taste of that visit is still with me, the sweetness that lasts only a moment, and the bitterness of a separation that is lost in the echo of an eternity. My heart yearns for the sight of your eyes. Your eyes are holding a flower stem and on their shores love lights up in fireworks. These eyes start to grow bigger and become the soul of the world. They conquer everything. They invest everything with the meaning of hope and love. From behind the rainy glass pane, my heart beholds the eternity of these ethereal eyes, and I live with the meaning that these eyes exude. An untenable moment of a visit—hours and days cast the die and I am separated from those eyes. Hey! Lady! Beautiful! Owner of those eyes! I bow to you from here, from this distance, and kiss your eyes. Say hello to Mamani. I love you as much as there are rain drops in this world.

FROM HOME

Hello, my husband! Last night rain was pouring and I thought that I love you as much as every single drop. Today, it is sunny and the air is clear. I think I like you more than this sun. And I was also thinking that it would've been nice for the rain and the sun to pour and shine on the doors of that prison official who is supposed to sign your release papers. Maybe the sun and the rain can soften his hands and make them realize the power of our love. "Free to go," he shall write. I live in the hope of that news. I want to have the strength to live when you come out. By the way, sir, did you see what your terrible handwriting did?[40] Sir, you better work on that handwriting of yours. I LOVE YOU.

---

40 On top of this letter, someone had written: "Write more clearly, otherwise it won't be sent." That person's handwriting or manners weren't pretty, of course.

Letter IX

Lady of the sonnet, o you sonnet of all romantic son-
nets! I greet you. I grow old like the year that is coming
to an end. I have passed the autumn to reach the beginning of the last year of my thirties. My hair is getting
white. Old age is extending its hands. But its territory
is limited. It cannot reach my heart. My heart is young.
Actually, it is a child, a playful child, a restless child in
whose restlessness you make a show, like the taste of a
sonnet by Hafez that possesses the quality of your eyes.
You stroll in it. Oh you sonnet, you love sonnet of my
life, you circulate in my blood, and you refresh me with
every cycle. Your eyes, lady of the sonnet, compose
poems in my heart to give me love and hope. These
poems laugh at the hopelessness of old age; I murmur
them continuously. I love you, fair lady, sonnet of my
life, I love you. Give my regards to Mamani.

FROM HOME

My man, my old man! It seems like yesterday when they took you away. When you left I was young. My face bore no wrinkles. I thought old age was a disease that some people were inflicted with. When the month of Bahman arrives, it will be six years since we were separated. My face is wrinkly and I now think that old age is an inevitable test designed for every human being. Darling, we are in this together, but what's there to fear? It may be true that we are racing towards old age but we are also ripe to the point that even if they grant us a day to live, we shall repeat the efflorescence of all springtime saplings, and nothing is more pleasant than old people who live young. I LOVE YOU.

Letter X

FROM PRISON

Lady, my precious lady! I greet you. Last night it snow-ed. I remembered you, thinking that you are perhaps anxious. I became anxious and I was depressed. The seventh winter of our separation is upon us and I still yearn to warm my heart in the rays of your solar eyes. How many long days and years have elapsed—and we are still separated. This is an enormous misfortune. Nevertheless, lady, your 39-year old man keeps his heart warm in this winter—with the thought of your smile and your eyes, and yearns for that day when "goodbye" will no longer be the end of our being together. I love you as much as there are seconds in these 39 years, and I count the seconds until the time when I come home. Say hello to Mamani. I LOVE YOU. I LOVE YOU. I LOVE YOU.

My 39-year old man, my old man! Greetings! I have heard of many people who have trodden a difficult path and, before reaching their destination, have doubted the journey. We are not supposed to be like those people. We mustn't be. Darling, I have said this many times: Every day of our lives has been fuller than the entire lifetime of most people. Therefore, let's promise not to give in to melancholy. Let's not begin to regret things. Let's be proud of our lives. Let's keep our hearts warm, as you suggested, with the help of this enormous love. Let's not at any point allow the power of this love to be tainted by sadness. I have never thought myself separated from you. You have been close to me even when behind bars. I have learned how to be with you. I LOVE YOU. Mamani loves you as well.

Letter XI

FROM PRISON
My generous lady, lady of reason and love and hope! I greet you. Eleven years have elapsed since you finally said YES to my petition and made the winter of my life forever a spring. Looking back at these years, I see that I have brought you nothing but suffering, and you have withstood this suffering with strength, kindness, and pride. You have suffered, with smiles and tears. I ask for forgiveness. I have made you suffer tremendously. Seventeen years ago, you were a lachrymose, sentimental young woman and today you are a wise lady that the world envies. I am fortunate that the blossoms of your love blooms in my eyes. In the anniversary of our love, like always, I come to you from every direction imaginable. And I lay before your feet all the wild flowers of the world. I strongly hope that this will be my last letter from prison and for this Bahman to become springtime for us. I LOVE YOU.

Afterword

Nooshabeh Amiri

In the Iranian historical memory the 1980's is the decade of great terror. It is an important and determining chapter in the history of what became known as the Islamic Revolution (with an emphasis on Islamic rule, today on its fourth decade). The 1980's started with the elimination and defecation of a rainbow of political groups that had formed in the wake of the Revolution, and ended with the mass execution and forced self-denunciation of political prisoners in 1988.

The Iranian Revolution of 1979 was the last major upheaval of the 20th century and in line with the popular French and Russian revolutions. It succeeded in unseating twenty five hundred years of monarchy in one of the oldest civilizations on this planet. It followed a century of popular struggle for a more participatory form of government. It was a broad based outburst that set for itself two main objectives: Freedom from a millennia of autocracy on a national level and from centuries of colonialism on an international level.

Many ideologies and political proclivities—fundamentalist, nationalist, liberal, Marxist—converged to bring the revolutionary force home. Ultimately, however, a grand cleric, Ayatollah Ruhollah Khomeini, became the revolution's grand representative, and under his command Mohammad Reza Pahlavi, the last Shah of Iran, was ousted; with a nod from Western powers. It was on January 3, 1979 in Guadeloupe that the Ayatollah promised Western countries in attendance that the flow of oil would continue if and when the popular revolt came to fruition. He also promised Iranians a new era of democratic openness.

Still outside the country, having just moved to Paris from Najaf in Iraq after 14 long years of exile, Ayatollah Khomeini told me when I interviewed him as a journalist: "Islam doesn't tolerate dictatorships. Marxists are also free to proclaim their ideologies." Once the revolt turned into the February 1979 Revolution, however, that enfranchising spirit was lost. What was labeled "the First Spring of Freedom" became the Last. Despite the Ayatollah's repeated assurances to the contrary, clerics got to occupy nodes of power in the "Islamic" state and quickly moved to implement the legal basis for a rule based on Islamic mandates or Sharia laws. A large swath of those who had helped in bringing the revolution about saw themselves as outsiders to those laws.

The reign of terror started with the enforcement of a dress code for women and moved to restrict political space. The ruling powers first targeted and arrested members of groups that had outwardly showed their opposition to the Islamic Republic. Styled after Stalinist show trials, members of opposition groups were paraded before cameras on television to denounce their beliefs and incriminate themselves and their organizations.

The outcome was that in a very short period of time Iranian citizens were divided into "revolutionary" and "anti-revolutionary." All those who had professed loyalty to the "sacred regime of Islamic Republic" were filed under the former and the rest tagged "corrupters of the earth;" an Islamic legal term carrying a sentence of death. The Islamic Republic thus legitimized any form of torture and punishment to be dealt to its critics and dissidents. It was based on these retributive show trials that the regime would eventually sentence the confessors to various terms of prison, or death. Prisoners carried next to no rights. Behind closed doors they had no recourse to legal representation. The court "jurist" had the power to decide the fate of prisoners based on his understanding of the Sharia laws.

In 1983 the circle of arrests and imprisonments widened to include groups that were faithful to the state but critical of it. Among these was the Tudeh Party, a Marxist-Leninist organization that followed the line suggested by the Soviet Union. It was the oldest and most organized political outfit in Iran. The Party backed the formation of the Islamic Republic in a March 1979 referendum, and stopped short of condemning its aggressive practices during the reign of terror. But the regime ultimately chose to even go after members of this party for reasons that are not yet clear to scholars. Some have suggested that the escape to London of a Tudeh member, who doubled as a KGB operative from within the Soviet Embassy in Tehran, gave the Iranian regime a pretext for this crackdown on Tudeh in February 1983.

Houshang Asadi was one of the writers of Tudeh's daily paper *Mardom* (The Masses) and among those arrested during the reign of terror. In *Letters to My Torturer: Love, Revolution and Imprisonment in Iran* (Oneworld Publications, UK 2010) Mr. Asadi paints a harrowing picture of the realities inside Islamic Republic prisons. Those arrested were subjected to a variety of psychological and physical torments to confess to being "spies." In the case of Mr. Asadi, he admitted—having been forced to eat his own excrement—to have been at once an agent of the KGB and the MI6. He was in solitary confinement and submitted to torture for more than two years without trial. During relocations he then ended up in Evin Prison and was capriciously sentenced to 15 years of prison. It was at Evin he first was given a piece of paper for correspondences, with no more than six lines.

Houshang Asadi was released in 1989, after six years of imprisonment. All prison visits had been canceled for a few months prior to the new round of summary trials. Political prisoners appeared before court only for a few minutes, and were asked only a few questions by the presiding judge: Do you denounce your political party? Do you believe in the Islamic Republic? Do you pray five times a day? Who is your *marja*?[41] That was it. Prisoners who gave the "wrong" answers were sentenced to death. Then the rest knew to give the expected answers to rescue themselves.

Our correspondence, alongside *Letters to My Torturer*, shed light on a dark era that plundered the lives of many, and the circumstances still remain locked in the chests of the victims. In a way, the 1980's was a bloody passage from a popularly conceived revolution to the birth of a zealously despotic regime. The many different religious groups that operated under the umbrella of the Islamic Republic midwifed the mass executions

---

41 In the Shia branch of Islam, believers should follow the wisdom of a sanctioned jurist, or *marja* (literally "reference") ayatollah.

of 1988. Interrogators, judges, and torturers who took part in the massacres were part and parcel of a regime that wanted to guarantee its survival at all possible cost. These letters were published at a time when the Republic was increasingly less tolerant of critics, some of which actually were an integral part of its parturition.

The six lines to and from prison—which were read closely by prison officials—were penned at some of the dreariest times in recent Iranian history. They nevertheless proclaim the victory of hope and love over forces of intolerance and doom.